MW00471476

The PARA Method

ALSO BY TIAGO FORTE

Building a Second Brain

The PARA Method

Simplify, Organize, and Master Your Digital Life

TIAGO FORTE

ATRIA BOOKS

NEW YORK   LONDON   TORONTO   SYDNEY   NEW DELHI

ATRIA
BOOKS

An Imprint of Simon & Schuster, Inc.
1230 Avenue of the Americas
New York, NY 10020

First Atria Books hardcover edition August 2023

ATRIA BOOKS and colophon are trademarks of Simon & Schuster, Inc.

For information about special discounts for bulk purchases, please contact
Simon & Schuster Special Sales at 1-866-506-1949 or
business@simonandschuster.com.

The Simon & Schuster Speakers Bureau can bring authors to your live event.
For more information or to book an event, contact the Simon & Schuster Speakers
Bureau at 1-866-248-3049 or visit our website at www.simonspeakers.com.

Interior design by Maya P. Lim, mayaplim.com

Manufactured in the United States of America

1 3 5 7 9 10 8 6 4 2

Library of Congress Control Number: 2023937919

ISBN 978-1-6680-4556-5
ISBN 978-1-6680-4557-2 (ebook)

To my mother, Valéria,
whose patience and thoughtfulness
gave me the keys to unlock
the secrets of organizing

Contents

The PARA Method

How to Read This Book

Every word in this book is designed to do one thing: propel you forward into taking action.

As you read, highlight anything that strikes you as interesting, surprising, or especially relevant to you. Those highlights can be the first items you add to your new PARA system!

I've structured this book in three parts and included everything you need to know to get started in Part 1. I strongly recommend you stop there and try implementing PARA for yourself, which takes less than sixty seconds using the instructions I've provided.

Part 2 contains additional guidelines and best practices I've gathered from years of coaching people through adopting PARA. I suggest you set a reminder to come back to this part after a couple of weeks testing your system in the real world.

Part 3 contains "deep dives" on more advanced topics that my collaborators, clients, and students have found helpful, such as how to formulate a project list, how to adopt habits to stay organized, and how to use PARA to enhance your focus, among others. These chapters can be read as needed when you find yourself hungry for more guidance.

There was a time when I insisted on reading every book I picked up from beginning to end, without exception. I slogged through countless boring, irrelevant books before eventually realizing that this attitude is completely counterproductive. You don't get a prize for starting a book or finishing one. Books are not trophies to collect or evidence you've learned anything.

The only reward from reading a book like this one comes from *putting what you learn into practice*, and you can do that after you've read just the first five chapters.

To match your commitment with one of my own, I will make you five promises as to what will happen once you adopt PARA:

PROMISE #1:

You will stop wasting time looking for information:

You will know exactly where your most important notes and documents live, and how to find them in seconds.

PROMISE #2:

_____

You will gain greater focus on what matters most:

You will have greater clarity about what's important so you can intentionally move your life into alignment with your interests and goals.

PROMISE #3:

You will make things happen:

You will consistently finish what you start, beating procrastination and tapping into your past learning to make progress fast.

PROMISE #4:

Your creativity and productivity will soar:

You will have access to a playground of your own ideas to finally do the creative work that's been locked up inside you.

PROMISE #5:

You will beat information overload and FOMO:

The fear of missing out on a key piece of information will disappear and be replaced with the confidence that you have everything you need to get started.

Let's begin!

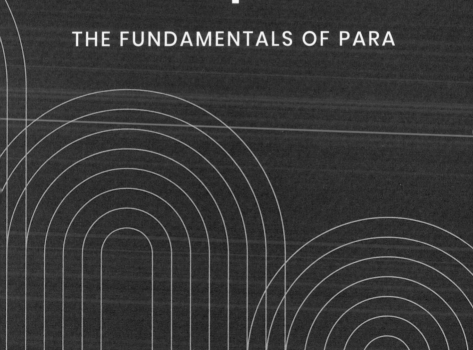

PART

1

THE FUNDAMENTALS OF PARA

1

Introducing PARA

Imagine for a moment the perfect organizational system.

A system that told you *exactly* where to put every piece of information in your digital life—every document, file, note, agenda, outline, and bit of research—and exactly where to find it when you needed it.

Such a system would need to be incredibly easy to set up, and even easier to maintain. After all, only the simplest, most frictionless habits endure long term.

It would need to be both flexible, adapting to your needs in different seasons of your life, and comprehensive, so you can use it in every one of the many places where you store information. For example, the Documents folder on your computer, a cloud storage platform,[1] or a digital notetaking app.[2]

But most of all, the ideal organizational system would be one that leads directly to tangible benefits in your career and life. It would dramatically accelerate you toward completing the projects and achieving the goals that are most important to you.

In other words, the ultimate system for organizing your life is one that is *actionable*.

Instead of putting more obstacles in your path, postponing the actions that will make a difference, it would pull those actions closer and make them easier to start and finish.

After more than a decade of personal experimentation, teaching thousands of students, and coaching world-class pro-

---

1 Commonly used cloud storage platforms include Microsoft OneDrive, Google Drive, Box, and Dropbox.
2 Popular digital notetaking apps include Notion, Evernote, Microsoft OneNote, Apple Notes, Google Keep, and Obsidian. You can find my full recommendations for which app to choose in our resource guide at buildingasecondbrain.com/resources.

fessionals, I've developed such a system. It's being used today by elementary schoolchildren all the way to multinational corporations, and everyone in between.

It's called PARA—a simple, comprehensive, yet flexible system for organizing any type of information across any digital platform.[3]

Whether you want to save excerpts from a book you're reading, a voice memo about an interesting new idea, inspiring quotes from a podcast interview, web bookmarks with useful online resources, notes from important meetings or phone calls at work, photos that remind you of cherished memories, or your own personal journal entries, this system will equip you with a set of tools for preserving any information far into the future. And not only preserving it, but skillfully using it to achieve anything you set your mind to.

---

3   *Para* is a Greek word that means "side by side," as in "parallel"; this reminds us that PARA works "side by side" with our brain to augment our memory and thinking.

Four Categories to Encompass Your Entire Life

PARA is based on a simple observation: there are only four categories that encompass all the information in your life.[4]

PROJECTS — Short-term efforts in your work or life that you're working on now

AREAS — Long-term responsibilities you want to manage over time

RESOURCES — Topics or interests that may be useful in the future

ARCHIVES — Inactive items from the other three categories

You have **projects** you're actively working on—short-term efforts (whether in your work or personal life) that you take on with a certain goal in mind. For example:

- Complete webpage design
- Buy a new computer

---

4   You can find a full list of common examples for each of the letters of PARA at buildingasecondbrain.com/para/examples.

- Write research report
- Renovate the bathroom
- Finish Spanish-language course
- Set up new living room furniture

You have **areas** of responsibility—important parts of your work and life that require ongoing attention more broadly. These might include:

- Work responsibilities such as Marketing, Human Resources, Product Management, Research and Development, Direct Reports, or Software Development
- Personal responsibilities such as Health, Finances, Kids, Writing, Car, or Home

Then you have **resources**[5] on a range of topics you're interested in and learning about, such as:

- Graphic design
- Organic gardening
- Web design
- Japanese cuisine

---

5   Alternative words for this category that some people have found more helpful are "reference" or "research."

- Photography
- Marketing assets

Finally, you have **archives,** which include anything from the previous three categories that is no longer active but you might want to save for future reference:

- Projects you've completed or put on hold
- Areas that are no longer active or relevant
- Resources that you're no longer interested in

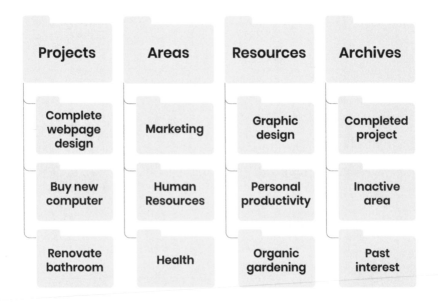

Projects	Areas	Resources	Archives
Complete webpage design	Marketing	Graphic design	Completed project
Buy new computer	Human Resources	Personal productivity	Inactive area
Renovate bathroom	Health	Organic gardening	Past interest

And that's it! Four top-level folders[6]—Projects, Areas, Resources, and Archives—each containing subfolders dedicated to each specific project, area of responsibility, resource, and archive in your life.

It may be difficult to believe that a complex, modern human life like yours can be reduced to just four categories. It may feel like you have far more to deal with than can fit into such a simple system. But that is exactly the point: if your organizational system is as complex as your life, then the demands of maintaining it will end up robbing you of the time and energy you need to live that life.

---

6   I will use the term "folder" to refer to the main unit of organization used by most software programs; some software instead uses directories, notebooks, tags, or links, which work just as well.

The system you use to organize information has to be so simple that it *frees up* your attention, instead of taking more of it. Your system must give you time, not take time.

The Key Principle—Organizing Information by Your Projects and Goals

Most of us first learned how to organize information in school. We were taught to categorize our class notes, handouts, and study material by *academic subject*, such as math, history, or chemistry.

Without realizing it, we took that same approach into adulthood. We continued to categorize our documents and files according to incredibly broad subjects like "Marketing," "Psychology," "Business," or "Ideas."

This makes zero sense in your postacademic career. In the workplace, there are no classes, no tests, no grades, and no diplomas. There is no teacher to tell you what to write down for the final exam, because there isn't one.

What you do have, both at work and in life, are *outcomes you are trying to achieve*. You are trying to launch a new product, come to a crucial decision, or reach a quarterly sales number. You are doing your best to plan a fun family vacation, publish a new piece of personal writing, or find affordable day care in your neighborhood.

In the midst of your busy day, as you are trying to make these things happen, you *absolutely do not have time* to go rummaging through a vast category like "Psychology" to find the article you saved six months ago.

Instead of organizing information according to broad subjects like in school, I advise you to organize it according to the projects and goals you are committed to right now.

This is what it means to "organize for action," a mantra I will return to throughout this book.

When you sit down to work on a graphic design project, for example, you will need all the notes, documents, assets, and other material related to that project all in one place and ready to go.

That might seem obvious, yet I've found it is exactly the opposite of what most people do. Most people tend to spread out all the relevant material they need to make progress in a dozen different places, which means they have to spend half an hour to locate them before they can even get started.

How do you make sure that all the material related to each project or goal is all in one place? You organize it that way in the first place. That way you know exactly where to put everything and exactly where to find it.

Your goals are that much closer to being achieved when all the information you need to execute your vision is right at hand. Let's find out what you're capable of achieving when the obstacles to that vision disappear.

2

The Power of Organizing by Project

started my career as a productivity coach in the San Francisco Bay Area in the early tens. It was the peak of the tech boom, and high-powered professionals from some of the world's most influential companies were looking for any edge in their performance. I was happy to oblige.

I coached several executives at a well-known biotech firm in South San Francisco, on a beautiful campus overlooking the bay. I remember one spring day I was waiting for my next client, a senior director in charge of developing several new lifesaving pharmaceuticals.

Once he arrived, our coaching session started with a simple question of mine: "Do you have a project list?"

When working with a client as a productivity coach, one of the first things I always ask them is to show me their project list. I need it to get a sense of what kind of work they do, their current workload, and what priorities and outcomes they are trying to move forward.

He said, "Sure!" and, after jotting down a quick list from memory (the first red flag), handed me a list like this:

My project list:

1. Hiring/staffing
2. Events
3. Direct reports
4. Strategic planning
5. Research
6. Vacations
7. Professional development
8. Productivity

Do you see the problem? Look again closely.

Not a single item on this list is a project, according to my definition. Projects are "short-term efforts," which means they need a clear end date. Does "strategic planning" ever end for good? Is there ever a time when you can permanently cross off "vacations" from your list? Hopefully not!

Every item on this list is, in fact, an area of responsibility—they continue indefinitely. This isn't just semantics. I've learned that no matter how smart or driven you are, there are two critical things you cannot do until you break down your areas of responsibility into specific, concrete projects.

OBSTACLE #1:
You Can't Truly Know the Extent of Your Commitments

One of the most common complaints I hear from people is that they "have no bandwidth." And I sympathize—how much of the time does it feel like you have way too much on your plate?

But as long as you view your work through the lens of areas, you'll never quite know *just how much* is on your plate. Looking at the list above, how much of a workload does "Hiring" represent? It could be anything from making a part-time hire every six months to filling fifty full-time positions this quarter.

There's simply no way to know at a glance, and that uncertainty will manifest itself as every area feeling more burdensome than it really is.

Imagine if you identified each of the projects *within* Hiring and kept that list in front of you every day. Wouldn't it be so much easier to tell how much there is to do and what you should do next? For example:

Hiring projects:
1. Hire for "Engineering Manager" position
2. Hire for "Project Analyst" position
3. Hire for "Marketing Director" position
4. Hire for "Field Researcher" position
5. Hire for "Financial Manager" position

You Can't Connect Your Current Efforts to Your Long-Term Goals

One of the most challenging (yet also rewarding) aspects of knowledge work is that it requires our creativity. And creativity can't really be sustained without a sense of motivation. You can't keep doing your best thinking and contributing your best ideas if you're burned out and demoralized.

What does our motivation depend on? Mostly, on making consistent progress. We can endure quite a bit of stress and frustration in the short term if we know it's *leading somewhere.*

Which brings us to our second problem: without a list of individual projects, you can't connect your current efforts to your long-term goals.

Look at the original list above again. None of the items on it will end or change—that's the definition of an area of responsibility, that it continues indefinitely. Now imagine the psychological effect of waking up week after week, month after month, and even year after year to the exact same list of never-ending responsibilities. No matter how hard you work, the endless horizon never seems to get any closer.

Honestly, I couldn't design a better way to kill motivation if I tried.

When you break down your responsibilities into bite-size projects, you ensure that your project list is constantly turning over. This turnover creates a cadence of regular victories that you get to celebrate every time you successfully complete a project. Imagine how motivated and accomplished you'd feel by breaking out a broad area like "Events" into each individual event you're organizing:

Event projects:

1. Quarterly staff retreat
2. Annual stakeholder conference
3. Workshop on research methods
4. End-of-year hiring fair
5. Executive summer retreat

No matter how wide-ranging your responsibilities are, you can *always* break them down into smaller projects...

...and you must, if you want to know whether you're actually making progress toward your goals.

Getting Organized for the Life You Want to Lead

Using PARA is not just about creating a bunch of folders to put things in.

It is about identifying the structure of your work and life—what you are committed to, what you want to change, and where you want to go. It is about organizing information in such a way that it supports and calls into being the future life you want to lead.

So much of what we call "organizing" is essentially procrastination in disguise. We tell ourselves we're "getting ready" or "doing research," pretending like that means progress.

In reality, we are seeking any little thing we can polish or tidy to avoid having to face the task we are dreading.

PARA cuts through this facade, giving us a method for organizing anything that is so radically simple, there is no excuse and nothing left to do except the next essential step. It is a minimalistic way to add *just enough* order to your environment that you have the clarity to move forward, and no more.

In the next couple of chapters, let's dive a little deeper into what it looks like to use this method to transform your digital life.

3

The Sixty-Second PARA Setup Guide

Y ou might think the first step of implementing PARA is to meticulously create all the individual folders you need within all four categories, and then individually move every one of your existing files into them.

In the past, I would spend many hours with my clients helping them do exactly that, but through trial and error I've found that is exactly the wrong way to start. Before you can create anything new, you have to clear out the old.

In this chapter, I'll walk you through the three steps I recommend you take to adopt PARA on any digital platform:

- Step 1: Archive existing files
- Step 2: Create project folders
- Step 3: Create additional folders as needed

I recommend starting with just one platform at first, such as the Documents folder on your computer, since it is typically the oldest and largest repository of information for most people.

STEP 1:

Archive Existing Files

In the physical world, every piece of paper, manila file folder, and object takes up precious space. Therefore, you have to make a decision about what to do with each and every one of them, even if that decision is simply to throw it away.

But the digital world is different. Digital objects don't take up any physical space; they take up *digital* space, which these days is essentially unlimited. This means you never really have to throw anything away. You can keep it all.

This may seem like a blessing, but in fact it's a curse.

The problem with keeping everything is that it quickly starts to consume a resource even more scarce than physical space: your attention. Every time you see all those random files strewn across your computer desktop, Documents folder, cloud drive, or notes app, some of your mental energy gets drained away.

You may think you can close your laptop and just ignore it, but a small part of your brain will continue worrying about the chaotic state of your digital environment until you put it in order. From the perspective of your brain, your information environment is just as important as your physical one, and it won't let you rest as long as it feels uncertain and threatening.

You can keep everything, but you *can't keep it front and center in your attention*. It needs a place to go for safekeeping—one that is secure but completely "out of sight, out of mind" until you need it.

That place is the Archives. Think of it like "cold storage" for your digital life. By placing something there, it gets "frozen" in time in exactly the state you left it, ensuring you can access it again in the future without having to worry about it in the meantime.

Here's what I want you to do: select *all* the existing files, documents, folders, notes, etc. in your Documents folder (which may number in the hundreds or even thousands or more) and move them all at once into a new folder called "Archive [Today's date]."

Think of this folder as a time capsule preserving everything you had going on at this moment in time, while separating what was saved before today's date from what will be saved from this point forward.

Then, place this new dated archive folder inside another, larger folder titled simply "Archives," which will be the official home of all your archives going forward.

That's it! You're done with step one.

Create Project Folders

Now that your Documents folder is clear, it's time to begin anew. You've created a beautiful blank slate, and now we'll add a little bit of structure to store the new things you'll be saving there.

For the second step, start by creating a new folder called "Projects." This will be the official home of all your information related to projects (short-term efforts with a clear end goal) going forward. Inside that new folder, create a subfolder for each one of your active projects and title them with the name of each project.

Projects		
Complete webpage design	Buy new computer	Write research report
Renovate bathroom	Finish Spanish course	Set up new furniture

The reason we want to focus on projects next is that they are the endeavors you're actively working on right now. They are therefore, by definition, more likely to be timely and pressing. You can go ahead and start moving any documents, notes, or files you're actively working with into the appropriate project folders, but don't feel the need to do it up front or all at once.

For example, for a bathroom renovation project, you might have:

- Measurements of the bathroom's dimensions
- Photos of tile patterns and colors you might want to use
- Quotes from several contractors you've spoken with
- Details of the winning bid and a signed contract
- Budget spreadsheet to track spending

Even for a project being executed by someone else, there is still lots of information to keep track of!

STEP 3:
Create Additional Folders as Needed

In the past, I would advise people at this stage to also create new folders for each of the areas and resources they imagined they would one day like to use. I thought having all those folders ready to go would make it more convenient to save new things in the future, but I've since realized the error of my ways.

My lightbulb moment came when I was hired to work with a software development firm in Silicon Valley on organizing their shared cloud storage drive.

We brainstormed all the PARA folders they might want to use and created their entire PARA system in one day. It felt great! But in the following weeks and months, I heard a very different story. Every time the engineers were looking for something, they would encounter a perfectly titled folder that seemed to promise exactly what they were seeking, only to double-click on it and find it empty. We had created a labyrinth of tantalizing doorways leading to empty rooms, which only caused frustration and disappointment as they failed to find what they were looking for again and again!

This experience led me to form a new rule: never create an empty folder (or tag, or directory, or other container) before you have something to put in it.

Therefore, for your areas and resources, I recommend you hold off on creating any "speculative" folders until you're sure what you want to put in them. It takes only a moment to create a new folder anyway, so there's no reason to do it in advance. These two categories are less actionable, and therefore less important, so it's not critical that you have them completely fleshed out from day one.

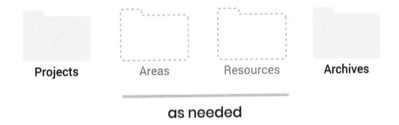

Projects   Areas   Resources   **Archives**

as needed

When you're ready, follow the same three steps above with your cloud storage drive, notetaking app, and anywhere else you store information, and your digital world will become a *para*dise (get it?) of simplicity and efficiency.[7]

---

7   See chapter 8 for more guidance on how to extend PARA across multiple platforms.

You now have a fully functional PARA system!

As you reorganize your digital life, I recommend taking this opportunity to reflect on how you want to change your attitude toward information going forward. Don't dump new stuff willy-nilly into your shiny new PARA folders, or you'll quickly find yourself right back in the chaos you had in the first place.

Think carefully about what you want to save in all four categories of PARA. What is truly unique or useful? What do you need in front of you when you sit down to focus on a project or area? Which resources are truly valuable, and which could you easily find again with a Google search?

This is your chance to wipe the slate clean and reboot your digital life based on timeless principles of organization.

What will you do with all the time and attention that get freed up as a result?

4

Five Key Tips for Making Organizing Easy

'␣ve now introduced you to the PARA Method and led you through the three steps of implementation.

Over the years as I've used this system to tackle all kinds of endeavors, I've discovered a few simple tips that make PARA even more effective and user-friendly. Each one requires only a onetime setup and a minute or two to implement.

TIP #1:
Create an Inbox

In the midst of a hectic week, you won't usually have time to perfectly capture, title, and file away new items as they arrive. Which means you need a separate time and place to "process" new items.

I recommend creating an additional, fifth folder alongside the four we've already covered, on each major platform you use (such as your Documents folder, cloud storage drive, and note-taking app) with the title "Inbox."

● ● ●
▶ **Inbox**
▶ **Projects**
▶ **Areas**
▶ **Resources**
▶ **Archives**

The inbox is a temporary holding area where new items accumulate until you have time to put them in their proper place.[8] In the next chapter I'll explain how to do that.

TIP #2:

Number the Folders

I suggest adding the numbers 0–4 at the beginning of the titles for each of the five folders you now have. Using "0" for the inbox reminds you that its contents have not yet been processed. This keeps them in the right order from most to least actionable when they are sorted alphabetically.

```
▸  0 Inbox
▸  1 Projects
▸  2 Areas
▸  3 Resources
▸  4 Archives
```

---

8 In many digital notetaking apps, an inbox (sometimes called a "daily notes" page) comes as a built-in feature. In others, you'll need to create it yourself.

Most of the time, you'll only look in folder #1, Projects. From time to time, you'll open up folder #2, Areas, when you want to think longer term. Folders #3 and #4, Resources and Archives, can remain safely out of sight until you need them.

TIP #3:
Use a Naming Convention

It's helpful if you can see a folder—on any platform, on any device—and instantly know which of the four main PARA categories it is in.

I like to use an informal naming convention to make this possible, such as:

- Emojis at the beginning of titles for project folders
- Capitalized titles for area folders
- Uncapitalized titles for resource folders

For example, these are immediately recognizable as projects (because they start with emojis):

- Create sponsorship package
- Write article on new environmental standards
- Plan Mexico City vacation

These are clearly areas (because they are capitalized):

- Professional Development
- Financial Management
- Travel

And these are resources (because they are uncapitalized):

- piano songs
- slide presentations
- video assets

These naming conventions also have the benefit of working across any platform, since they require only the most basic text characters.

TIP #4:
Activate Offline Mode

PARA works flawlessly in "offline mode" for one simple reason: it puts all the material you'll most likely need access to on-the-go in one place—your Projects folder.

Rather than having to hunt down all the documents related to a given project in a dozen different places, they are already in one place. The Projects folder also happens to be the smallest in terms of required disk space—only about 1 percent of all my digital notes, for example, live under "Projects"—which makes it easy to download them to your local device when you know you won't have Internet access but still need access to your information.

Take a minute to activate offline mode for just the Projects folder (and its subfolders) on each device you use while traveling, in transit, or when you just want to shut off the Wi-Fi and focus.[9]

TIP #5:
Make Backups

Since you're investing significant time and effort organizing your digital world, that world is going to be a lot more valuable. To ensure that effort doesn't go to waste, I recommend creating a reliable backup system for each of the main platforms you use (since each one will contain different information).

---

9   Depending on which software you're using and your available disk space, this might include turning on a setting called "Available offline" for the folders you want to download, turning on "Local sync" for all your files, or another feature.

If you're using a cloud-based platform of any kind, this step is already taken care of since all your data is stored in the cloud. For the files on your computer, you can use a cloud backup service (which will initiate backups automatically when you're online) or set a reminder to regularly back up to an external hard drive.

Customizing Your PARA System

You probably already have a shining image in your mind of what life will be like once you're living the PARA lifestyle. And I sincerely hope it all comes true. But if you falter at any point along the way, come back to this spot in the book. I know that life often gets hectic, so PARA is designed to "fail gracefully" in a couple of different ways.

First, it doesn't matter where you put a given file or note. If you find that the "filing" of items is too mentally taxing or time-consuming, don't worry too much about it. You'll likely be retrieving information using the search function most of the time, which means placing items into specific subfolders is a nice-to-have, not a must-have.

You'll see in chapter 9 that you will have many opportunities in the future to "flow" items between categories, so the decision of where to put something in the first place is very forgiving. There are backup plans and safety nets at every stage.

Second, it doesn't matter that you have exactly four PARA categories. Believe it or not, even the four main folders described by the letters of PARA are optional. I've seen people who prefer more and add an extra letter for an additional category of information (such as *S* for "Systems" or *V* for "Values"). I've also seen people make do with only two, such as a "Hot" folder for anything currently actionable and a "Cold" folder for everything that's not.

The important principle is to separate out whatever is most actionable and timely and give it the majority of your attention, and there are countless ways to do so. Don't feel the need to follow my prescriptions exactly—I give you permission to customize.

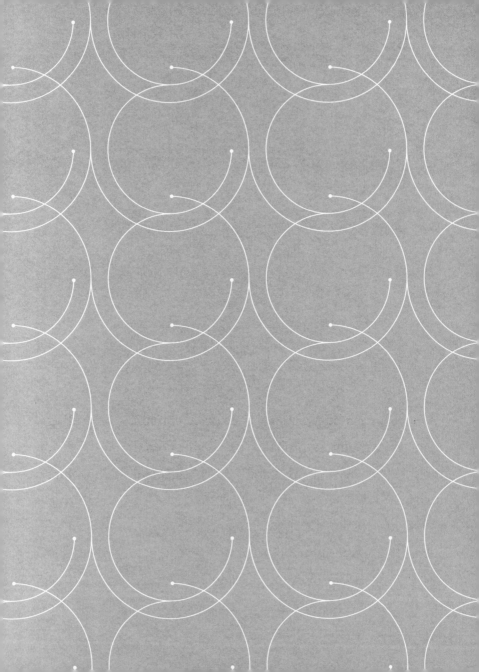

5

How to Maintain Your PARA System

I know you're a busy person with a rich, varied life, and filing your documents is probably not high on your priority list, nor should it be. I'm the same—I want to spend the absolute minimum amount of time possible tweaking and optimizing my system.

For that reason, I recommend you do all the upkeep of your PARA system in just five minutes per week. All you need to do is follow these three easy steps:

1. Retitle new items in your inbox

2. Sort new items into PARA folders

3. Update your active projects

Let's take a closer look at each one.

STEP #1:
Retitle New Items in Your Inbox

In a typical week, I accumulate around ten to twenty new digital items in my inbox. They might include notes from a team meeting, highlights from a book I'm reading, a useful screenshot from a website, or a voice memo I recorded about a new idea, for example.

When they are initially created, these kinds of files normally have a useless title like "Untitled document" or "New note." I find that it aids future retrieval tremendously if I take a few seconds to look at each item I've saved and change its title or name to something more informative and clear.

For example:

- Meeting notes with Clara 3/2/23

- Highlights from book *The Oxygen Advantage*

- Useful website on how to do hiring interviews
- Voice memo on new online course idea

There's nothing fancy or technical about these names. Sometimes I include a date, and sometimes I don't. All I'm doing is giving each item the shortest, simplest, easiest-to-understand title I can think of within a few seconds.

Note that you likely have several inboxes you'll need to do this for, such as:

- An inbox you've created in your Documents folder (recommended in chapter 4)
- An inbox for your cloud storage drive
- An inbox in your digital notetaking app

STEP #2:
Sort New Items into PARA Folders

The second step of "processing" any new items is moving them into the appropriate PARA folders. This also takes just a few seconds each, as I consider in which project, area, or resource a given document will be most relevant and useful.

Where to put a piece of information?

Follow this flowchart to find where best to store it.

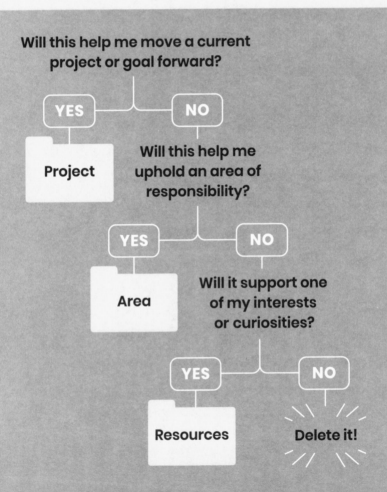

By doing all this "filing" in one batch, I find I can easily process my ten to twenty new items in just a few minutes. Since I'm most likely to find them again using search, the decision of where to put them is low stakes. I also find that briefly revisiting new information I've captured over the last week serves as a helpful reminder of any follow-up actions I need to take.

STEP #3:
Update Your Active Projects

Finally, take a look at your project folders and make changes to reflect what's happened over the past week. This could include actions such as:

- Changing the name of a project to reflect a new scope or direction
- Splitting a large project into smaller ones to make it more achievable
- Archiving a project that has been completed, put on hold, canceled, or handed over to someone else
- Unarchiving a dormant project that has since become active again and moving it back to the Projects folder

Before archiving a project, scan it briefly for any material (such as brainstorms, background research, slides, interview notes, etc.) that might be relevant to other pursuits and move these items to the appropriate place within PARA.

For example, let's say you discover a new strategic framework during a client engagement and, once it's finished, decide you'd like to utilize that knowledge with future clients. You could move that documentation to a new resource folder called "Strategy," which you'll be able to refer to again in the future.

All you're doing in this step is changing the makeup of your project folders to accurately reflect whatever has happened in your world recently.

There is tremendous power in changing your organizational system to fit your evolving needs and goals, instead of trying to force your needs and goals to fit your system.

Always Start with the Archives

The biggest misconception I see about the pivotal act of "archiving" is that you're never going to see that information again.

Don't think of the Archive as an "idea graveyard" where information goes to die. Your archives represent the sum total of your life experience, a treasure trove of hard-won lessons and profound insights you've gained from both successes and failures alike. I guarantee it will contain useful material you can reuse and recycle in future endeavors.

The Archive should be your starting point any time you launch a new project, do a personal year-end review, or update your résumé for a new job. It contains the supporting evidence you'll need to successfully advocate for a raise or promotion, pitch a new client, or propose a bold new venture.

I'm constantly surprised how frequently I find useful material from the past—notes on a conference call with a repeat client, background research on an industry, or photos I saved for design inspiration—all of which represents my personal "knowledge capital."

Reusing these knowledge assets not only saves me tremendous amounts of time—it makes me feel like I'm starting a marathon at the halfway point, instead of at the starting line like everyone else.

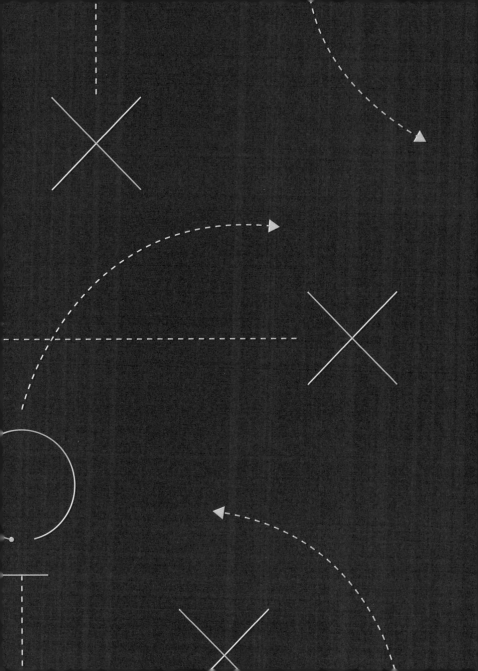

PART

2

THE PARA PLAYBOOK

6

How to Distinguish between Projects and Areas

S oon after I landed my first professional job in my midtwenties, I picked up a book called *Getting Things Done*. Written by executive coach and consultant David Allen, it presented an approach to personal productivity that was systematic and principled.

That approach is known as GTD, and it immediately had a dramatic impact on how I worked. It was like putting on X-ray glasses: suddenly I could see the information flowing toward me in terms of clear categories, each one designed to make it easier to *act* on that information.

Of the many definitions and distinctions that Allen introduced me to, perhaps the most powerful is between projects and areas (of responsibility). These are the two most actionable categories of information you encounter each day, and thus the most important to master.

I've noticed this is also a confusing and unclear distinction for many people. Let's take a closer look at each one through the lens of how they work within PARA.

Projects: A Goal with a Deadline

My definition of a project is any endeavor that has:

1. A **goal** that will enable you to mark it "complete"

2. A **deadline** or timeframe by which you'd like it done

A goal is simply "the outcome the project is trying to achieve." It could be a successful staff retreat, a website redesign, or a kid's birthday party—there is something you are trying to have happen in the real world that will enable you to mark it "complete."

A deadline adds a time limit to achieving your goal. You don't want your efforts lingering on forever, never quite knowing whether you succeeded or failed. Having some kind of end point in mind (whether strict and externally imposed or informal and self-imposed) allows you to ask yourself, "How much can I get done with the time remaining?"

Areas of Responsibility: A Standard to Maintain over Time

While projects are important, not everything is a project.

There are facets of your work and life that don't have a clear end goal or deadline. We call them "areas of responsibility."

An area of responsibility has:

1. A **standard** to be maintained

2. An **indefinite** end date

Work-related areas include your job duties, whether that is management, customer service, financial analysis, strategy, coaching, direct reports, or advising. You also have areas of responsibility in your personal life, like your health, finances, personal development, and relationships, which will continue in some form for as long as you live.

In all the examples above, the areas have no particular outcome to be achieved. There is no finish line you can reach that allows you to "complete" your health, or "finish" strategy once and for all, or "check off" finances as an ongoing concern.

Instead of a goal, an area of responsibility has a *standard you're trying to maintain.*

For example, if you're responsible for an area at work like leading product development, there is a standard of performance (or a "quality bar") for the product you are responsible for. That may include upgrading its speed and performance, fixing bugs quickly, and approving new updates to be released.

For your finances, your standard may be that you pay all your bills on time and provide for your family's needs. For parenting, it may be that you spend quality time with your kids every evening and make sure they are always loved and protected.

Maintaining your areas is an ongoing process. It requires thoughtfulness and self-awareness to sense what you want and what's missing in each one. An area is not so much a prize to win as a dance to enjoy. This is the realm of daily habits, meaningful rituals, and timeless values that transcend any particular project.

Distinguishing Projects and Areas

To put it simply: projects end, while areas continue indefinitely.

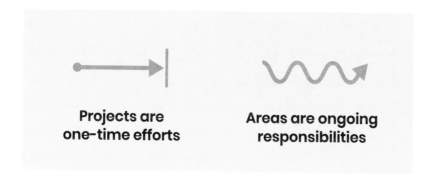

Projects are one-time efforts

Areas are ongoing responsibilities

However, there are a few other subtleties you should be aware of.

Every project typically falls under an area of responsibility. For example:

- Running a marathon is a project, which falls under the area of Health

- Publishing a book is a project, which falls under the area of Writing
- Saving three months' worth of expenses is a project, which falls under the area of Finances
- Planning an anniversary dinner is a project, which falls under the area of your Spouse

Although projects and areas are related, it's critically important that you distinguish between them. Failing to do so is a root cause of so many frustrations and challenges. Let me illustrate why.

If you have a project (such as writing a book), but you treat it like an ongoing area, without any particular goal or outcome in mind, it will feel aimless and directionless. Likewise, if you have an area (like maintaining a certain weight), but you treat it like it's just a onetime project, then even if you succeed in losing the extra weight, you'll likely revert right back afterward because you didn't put in place long-term habits.

In other words, projects and areas require completely different approaches, mindsets, and tools to be successful. Knowing which ones to use starts with identifying them correctly in the first place.

Sprints versus Marathons

Think of projects as sprints—you are sprinting to reach the finish line as fast as possible. Areas are like marathons—you have to sustain a consistent level of performance over a long distance.

I've noticed most people tend to favor either projects or areas in the way they lead their lives. Does either description below sound familiar?

"Project people" are good at sprints. Give them a clear goal and a path to get there, and they will ferociously chase after it with everything they have. The weakness of sprinters is that once they've reached their goal, they will often have trouble keeping it going. Sprinters are prone to starting many things and getting obsessed for a short time, before moving abruptly to something else.

"Area people" excel at marathons. Send them on a long journey and they will doggedly keep at it for as long as it takes. The weakness of marathoners is that they often have trouble changing direction. When an opportunity opens up that requires quick, decisive action, marathoners might stubbornly maintain their current direction even when it no longer makes sense.

Once you view your life through the lens of projects and areas, it becomes very clear that you need both: sprints to ramp up something new, and marathons to sustain it. Projects bring you the novelty and excitement of starting new things, whereas areas bring you the peace of mind and sense of perspective you want at the end of the day whether you succeeded or not.

PARA is a support system for both—executing projects and maintaining areas—which is why those two categories are front and center in how I recommend you organize your digital life.

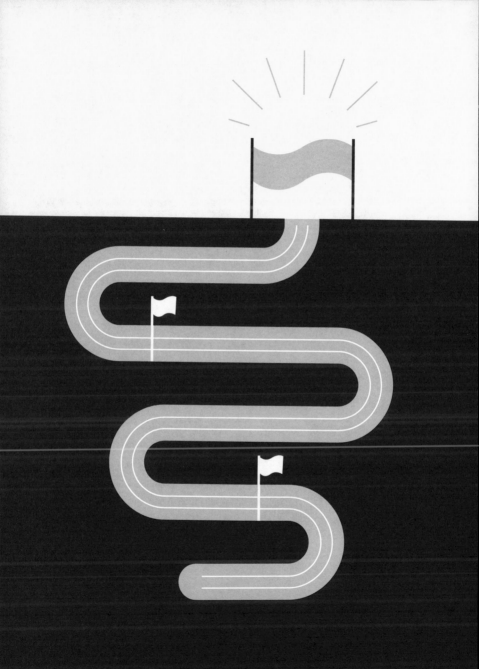

7

How to Distinguish between Areas and Resources

The second-most-important distinction within PARA is between Areas and Resources (the middle letters *A* and *R*).

At first glance, they might seem very similar, especially considering that a given topic (such as "Nonprofit fundraising" or "Nutrition research") could be located in either one.

It depends on *what that category of information means to you.*

If you are a public health professor at a major university, responsible for several lecture classes while also publishing your own research, then "Nutrition research" will definitely be an important area of responsibility for you.

But if you are a student at that same university, majoring in anthropology in another department, with nutrition as a minor side interest, then it will be a resource for you.

The key here is to realize that there is a big difference between *things you are directly responsible for* and *things you are merely interested in*. I use uppercase titles for areas and lowercase titles for resources to constantly remind myself that one is more important than the other.

Once again, any confusion between these two categories will produce a lot of friction and wasted energy.

Let's look at a few examples.

Areas: The Roles You Play and the Hats You Wear

Areas are parts of our lives that require ongoing attention to uphold a certain level of quality or performance. It's helpful to think of them as the "roles you play" or the "hats you wear" at work and in life.

At work, you have official roles you were hired to fulfill, such as Video Production, Legal Affairs, or Customer Service. There might also be unofficial responsibilities you've taken on over time, such as Company Newsletter, Mentoring, or Staff Retreats.

The same is true in our personal lives. We wear different hats even throughout the course of a single day: Spouse, Parent, Soccer Coach, Neighbor, or Friend. These roles tend to be more informal, but still involve a level of responsibility for us to uphold. A folder for "Spouse" might contain notes on their favorite restaurants, ideas for gifts, or health information you might need in case of an emergency. A folder for "Soccer Coach" might contain drills, practice schedules, and a team roster with contact information. Anything you might need to reference or remember in order to effectively play these roles is worth noting down.

Resources: Interests, Curiosities, and Passions

Resources encompass the vast number of things you might be interested in, curious about, or passionate about at any given time.

Resources can include new skills you're learning, such as breakdancing, photography, or golf. They could be fields or trends you're curious about, like parenting, cryptocurrency, or artificial intelligence. Resources can also include your hobbies and passions: woodworking, bread baking, or playing the piano.

Although you may feel a lot of enthusiasm for these pursuits, I recommend using the relatively cold word "resources" for a very specific reason. I am a naturally curious person with dozens, if not hundreds of different subjects I'd like to know more about. But I also know my tendency is to collect too much and become a "digital hoarder." I've found that I need a constraint to remind me what is worth saving and what isn't.

The word "resources" calls to mind the *utility* of a piece of information. Instead of asking, "Is this interesting?" which always results in overcollecting, I ask myself, "Is this *useful*?" That's a much higher bar and forces me to consider what this piece of information will allow me to do that I couldn't do otherwise, which problem it could help me solve, or which obstacle it might help me overcome.

Taking into account the importance of utility, resources can also include "assets" such as stock photos, product testimonials, code snippets, typography samples, or a "swipe file," a common practice from the advertising industry in which copywriters keep a folder full of examples to draw from in their work.

Areas Are Private Whereas Resources Are Shareable

There is an additional guideline that many people have found helpful in distinguishing what goes in Areas versus Resources: the boundary between private and shared information.

Areas of responsibility are inherently private. It's no one else's business what material you save related to your Health, Finances, Personal Growth, or Kids. For example, in my Health (area) folder, I keep blood panels, notes from doctor's visits, medical bills, and vaccination records (all things relevant only to me personally). I can always share an individual item if I want, but these categories should remain private by default.

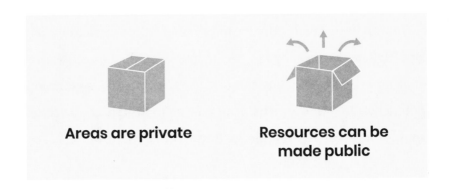

Areas are private   **Resources can be made public**

Resources are quite different, since learning and exploring new things are inherently social activities. There are many situations where you might want to share your notes with someone else—to get feedback on an article you're writing, to compare notes with a colleague on a skill you're both learning, or to offer restaurant recommendations to a friend who is visiting a city you've been to before.

Therefore, I recommend you think of your resource folders as "shareable by default." That way you can share individual documents (or even entire folders) with others on the fly, without first having to comb through them for any personal details.

An Opportunity to Be Completely Honest with Yourself

In my coaching, I often notice that people will pour a tremendous amount of time and effort into something they describe as a "side interest," while simultaneously neglecting critically important aspects of their lives, like their exercise, diet, relationships, or mental health.

We've all done it—some area of our lives feels too complex, uncertain, or confronting, so we throw ourselves at something else to take our mind off it. It feels great at first, distracting ourselves from pressing problems in favor of an exciting new hobby or research interest. It feels like the "new thing" is something we can understand and master and make tangible progress in.

But this story always ends the same way: as we ignore important areas of our lives, the costs and consequences start piling up, until one day the dam breaks. And then we are left to pick up the pieces, an experience so painful that it often restarts the whole cycle.

The line between areas and resources is an opportunity to be completely honest with yourself: What is inside the circle of your responsibilities, which no one else is going to take care of for you, and what is outside?

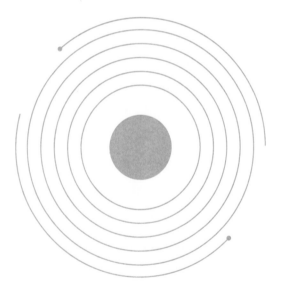

How can you take this chance to be more honest with yourself about which areas of your life need more attention, and organize your digital environment to support them?

8

Extending PARA across Multiple Platforms

O ne of the key features of PARA is that it's universal—it works across *every* platform where information can be stored, for *any* kind of information you might want to save, and is accessible on *any* device.

I notice that even the most organized people often make a fatal error—they use a different organizing system in each and every place where they keep information. Their to-do list is organized one way, their computer another, their cloud storage yet another, and their notes app...you get the picture.

This is problematic because every organizational system has *overhead*—a certain amount of cognitive effort required to maintain and use it. Even if each different organizing method makes sense in isolation, when combined, they create a crushing mental load that not even the world's smartest people can withstand.

In contrast, PARA is "platform agnostic," meaning it is *one system* that can be implemented everywhere, including:

- Your to-do list app
- Your computer file system (or Documents folder)
- Your cloud storage drive
- Your digital notetaking app
- Other platforms where information is stored

This universality allows you to "extend" the same PARA folders across every platform you use:

Here's why this is important: you will always need to use multiple platforms to do your work and live your life. Most projects you take on and areas you manage will involve different kinds of content, each of which needs to be stored on a platform that's suited to it.

For example, if you are publishing a research report on an emerging industry, you'll likely have data you're drawing on (which might be saved in a spreadsheet application), photos of popular products (which would be stored in a dedicated photo application), notes from your conversations with knowledgeable experts (saved in a notetaking app), PDFs of industry publications (in your Documents folder), and a list of next steps you're contemplating (in a to-do list app).

Technology is advancing too quickly on too many fronts for any one app to fulfill every need. Instead of fighting the tide and looking for "one app to rule them all," use as many apps as you like, while replicating the *same structure* across every single one. I recommend doing so down to the exact same spelling, punctuation, and capitalization so that you can mentally transition between platforms as seamlessly as possible. This way you can take advantage of the unique capabilities of each platform you might want to use, without sacrificing coherence and consistency in the way you relate to information.

PARA perfectly mirrors the structure of your life across every platform you use. Rather than forcing your life to fit into the opinions and preferences of whatever tool you happen to be using, I advise you to do the opposite: decide how you want to order your life and work, and then ask how your tools can support that.

How to Know Where to Put a Given Item

Since you'll have the same PARA categories across multiple platforms, the next obvious question is: How do I know on which platform a given item should be saved?

I use the following rules of thumb to tell me which digital storage medium is best for any given piece of information:

1. If it's an **appointment or meeting** happening at a specific time, it goes on my **calendar**

2. If it's a **task** that I can complete anytime, it goes in my **to-do list app**

3. If it's **text**, it goes in my **notetaking app** (since that offers the best search function by which to find it again)

4. If it's **content that I'll be collaborating on with others,** it goes in my **cloud storage drive**[10]

5. **If it can't go in any of the above locations** (because it's too large or a specialized file type, for example), then it goes in my **computer's file system** (the Documents folder)

Note that four of the platforms mentioned above are organized using PARA:

- To-do list app (projects and areas only, since these are the two categories that have tasks associated with them)[11]

- Notetaking app

- Cloud storage drive

- Computer file system

---

10 If you use a cloud productivity suite, such as Microsoft 365 (formerly known as Microsoft Office 365) or Google Workspace (formerly known as Google Suite), your cloud storage drive will be integrated with a full suite of productivity apps for word processing, spreadsheets, slide presentations, and more. In most cases all the documents you create or upload to such a cloud storage drive can be organized using PARA in the cloud.

11 Tasks are usually part of projects, but sometimes you can have a "free-floating" task that falls within an area and isn't part of any particular project. For example, "Correct typo on website" stands alone as part of a "Website" area.

My storage flowchart:

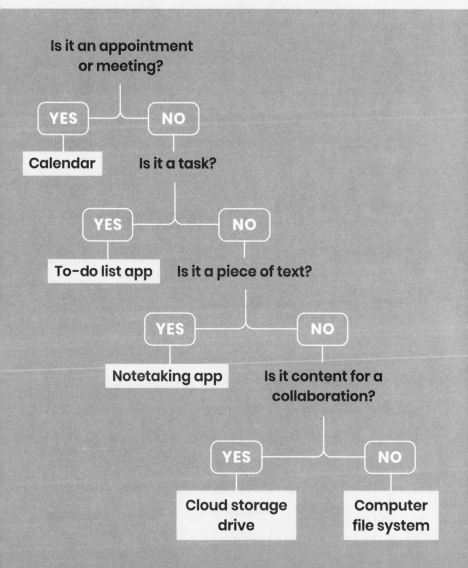

Whereas the calendar is time-based, so it makes more sense to organize it chronologically by date.

There is one exception to the above: if I want to save a sensitive piece of information—a tax document, credit card details, medical data, or passwords for example—I save it in an encrypted password manager app to make sure no one can access it except me.

The Benefits of a Cross-Platform System

At this point some people will wonder, "Do I really have to create corresponding, identical folders on all platforms?"

And the answer is: Absolutely not!

First, you should create a folder on any platform only when you have something to put in it. Otherwise, you'll just end up creating a maze of empty folders that clutter your workspace while leading nowhere. It takes mere seconds to create a new folder anyway, so you should do so only if and when it's needed.

Second, there is no reason that a given category should have corresponding folders across multiple platforms at all. For example, the recordings of my Zoom calls are automatically saved in a resource folder on my computer, but I certainly don't need a "Zoom recordings" folder elsewhere. Many categories of information can exist on only one platform—extend them across multiple platforms only if needed to move a project forward.

I know it may seem like a waste of time to manually create the same folders in the different places where you store information. It does take a little extra effort, but in return you gain a tremendous benefit: you are not stuck with any single platform.

I was once working on a major consulting project for a large telecommunications company, when without warning the project management platform we were using stopped working. They had been acquired by a large tech company, which had decided to shut down the product abruptly. While the rest of my team was in disarray, I was able to pivot to a new platform within minutes because my projects and areas already existed independently of any particular software program.

The landscape of productivity software is always changing, but that doesn't mean your organizing methods have to be. If a feature you depend on stops working, or the policies or pricing of a platform unexpectedly change, that affects only one platform. With PARA, any risk or vulnerability is limited to just one part of your digital life and doesn't automatically knock out all the others.

PARA is a cross-platform system for one simple reason: your projects are cross-platform. You'll rarely use just one app to bring a project to completion. PARA provides a way to tie together the information you'll need to access even though it's stored in multiple places.

Imagine what would be possible if the multiplicity of software tools you use wasn't a problem, because they all worked together in harmony with each other.

How would your
work change if every
tool at your disposal
was propelling you
forward and easing
the path toward
the future you want
to create?

9

Keep Information Flowing

One of the most common questions people have as they begin discovering the power of PARA is about the future: "What do I have to do to keep this system going?"

And this is where PARA truly shines, because the answer is: not much.

There are no strict rules about which format information has to be in—it can be text documents, images, PDFs, audio or video files, slide presentations, GIFs, or anything else. There are no

rules about how the items you save must be named—a straightforward title describing what it is works fine.

And there are no rules about the internal organization of
folders, which is where you can really waste a lot of time—each
subfolder of PARA can have its contents sorted chronologically
by date created if you want, but your computer can easily handle
that without your involvement.

So what is left for us to do?

The answer is that *you have to keep the information moving.*

PARA isn't a mechanical system like a car engine that needs
very precise and regular maintenance. It's more like an organic
system such as a pond or a forest. The same way a pond will
begin to stagnate and smell if the water isn't flowing, your PARA
system will soon go out of date and lose relevance if the knowledge it contains stops flowing.

Flows of Information within PARA

Most approaches to organizing are *static*: they assume that there
is one correct place for a given piece of information. You may
recall the Dewey decimal system from your local library, with a

precise call number telling you *exactly* where on the shelf each book goes.

But when it comes to *personal* organization of *digital* information, there is no such "correct" place. PARA is a dynamic system: any given file or document can go in any number of places—what matters is *your relationship to it*. And that relationship is changing all the time.

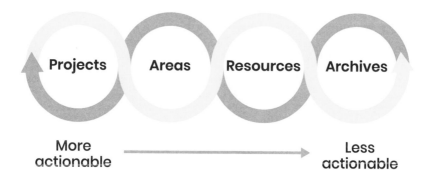

Projects **Areas** **Resources** **Archives**

More actionable → **Less actionable**

To illustrate this, imagine you read an article about effective coaching techniques one evening and save a few of the best excerpts to your notetaking app. Perhaps at that moment in your career, you are an individual contributor and don't have an immediate need for advice on how to coach other people in a professional setting. You file away this note in a resource folder called "coaching" for future reference.

The next year, you get promoted to a management position in your company and now have a handful of direct reports to manage. In the blink of an eye, that whole category of knowledge has suddenly become *actionable*.

You might take several decisive steps in your PARA system to reflect your new role. Those notes about coaching techniques might get moved from a resource folder on "coaching" to a new area folder called "Direct Reports." You've now *promoted* that knowledge so that it receives more of your attention on a more frequent basis.

Now imagine a couple more years pass, and you're promoted once again to a senior executive role. Once again, the landscape of your knowledge gets remapped. You might now be responsible for creating management training to teach all the new managers in the company what you've learned.

The contents of your "Direct Reports" area folder might now flow into a new project folder called "Management training workshop," as the knowledge it contains is now most relevant to the near-term goal of delivering your first workshop. The insights and ideas you collected years ago during an evening of casual reading have now bubbled up to the surface and become relevant to your most pressing challenge.

Finally, imagine a couple more years pass, and you've decided to quit your day job and start a business of your own. The notes you've saved in your "Management training workshop" project folder are now no longer actionable, as you don't expect to have employees to manage for a while.

There's no need to delete anything—just move it to the Archives. When the day eventually arrives that you start hiring your own staff, that knowledge will be ready and waiting like a dormant volcano, ready to spew forth a career's worth of wisdom.

Can you see how all it takes is one event in our lives to completely reshape the landscape of our priorities? At that point, we don't have time to "do more research"—we need to *already have done* that research through our reading and notetaking.

The contents of PARA are constantly flowing between different categories as your needs, goals, lifestyle, and priorities shift.

There is nothing as constant as change in today's world, which is why we need to avoid rigid systems that encourage a fixed mindset toward information.

Keep the Information Flowing

Here are some other examples of situations in which a specific piece of information (whether a single line of text, a photo, a digital note, or an entire folder full of documents) might flow between PARA categories.

From **PROJECTS to AREAS:** You might find that a training plan you used to prepare for a marathon (a project) is something you'd like to become a routine. You can create a new area folder called "Exercise" and move it there so that it remains an ongoing part of your life.

From **AREAS to PROJECTS:** If you decide it's time to level up operations within your organization (which will require a onetime project), the perfect place to start is with any ideas you've collected in an "Operations" area folder. New projects often emerge out of existing areas of responsibility.

From **AREAS to RESOURCES:** Sometimes, you realize that a piece of information you initially thought was relevant only to you (such as a list of event venues in a city) could also provide value to others. Move it from areas to resources, where it will be ready to share.

From RESOURCES to AREAS: Let's say you decide to start cooking at home more to improve your health and nutrition. A perfect way to start would be to move a few easy-to-make recipes from a "recipes" resource folder to your "Cooking" area folder. That way you can get started quickly without getting distracted by "doing more research" on the Internet.

From AREAS and RESOURCES to ARCHIVES: We've already discussed how projects go into the Archives when they are completed or put on hold. The same is true for areas and resources: if you lose interest in bird-watching, chess, jiu-jitsu, or motorcycle repair, there's no need to delete all that content. Just move it to the Archives in case it ever becomes relevant again.

From ARCHIVES to PROJECTS: Imagine you want to organize a conference to establish your company's thought leadership in a new industry. A lot of the planning and materials for conferences are similar and can be reused, provided you've saved them. Do a search for a professional event you've organized in the past, and you can move any useful materials you find there to a new project folder to reuse all that past knowledge.

One final note: though my preferred method is to move notes and files wholesale from one place to another, you actually have four options for how to associate an existing piece of information with a new category:

1. Moving a single item (if only one item is relevant to a new project, for example)
2. Moving a folder full of items (if a whole group of items is relevant)
3. Linking two items together (if you want to keep the original item where it is)[12]

---

12 Most digital notetaking apps and file storage platforms offer the ability to create "links." You can use that feature to create links between documents on the same platform, or even between documents located on different platforms.

4. Tagging items with the same tag (if you want to associate
   many items with each other without moving them)

The only action I recommend avoiding at all costs is duplication: you never want to have two versions of a file or document, because then you never know which one is the most current.

The purpose of keeping your information moving is to keep yourself moving. When the information around you is constantly flowing and changing, you'll find it's much easier to see problems from a new perspective and avoid getting bogged down. You'll even find that projects get going before you even realize you've started them!

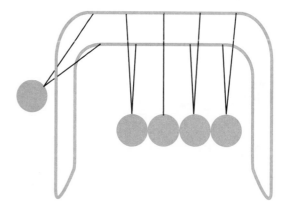

10

Using PARA with a Team

O
ur digital worlds are constantly colliding with and overlapping with the digital worlds of others.

Knowledge is meant to be shared, which means you may already be wondering whether you can use PARA to collaborate with others. The good news is that PARA works just as well for teams, companies, and other organizations as it does for individuals!

I've consulted with and trained hundreds of people from various industries on how to organize their knowledge, from multibillion-dollar financial institutions like the World Bank to leading biotech firms like Genentech to innovative start-ups like Sunrun.

We all operate in a knowledge-based economy now, which means the ability to document and access what your people know is crucial not only for growth, but for survival.

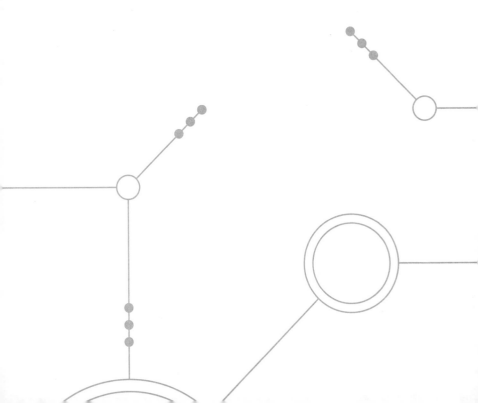

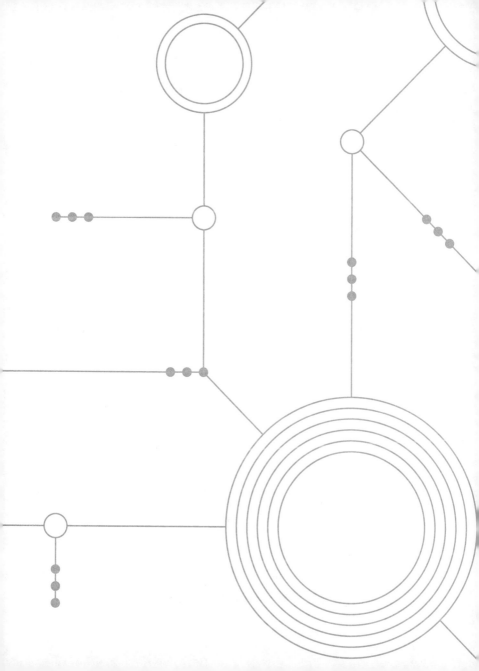

A Bottom-Up Approach to Knowledge Management

PARA is part of a decades-old field called "Knowledge Management," or KM for short. The purpose of KM is to find ways for people to effectively share their knowledge with each other to advance an organization's goals.

I distinctly remember the time an executive at a company where I once worked decided to "implement" Knowledge Management one day out of the blue. A wiki (or knowledge base) was created, and we were told to "share our knowledge" by inputting what we were learning into it. After the first couple of weeks, no one ever looked at it again.

That experience and other similar ones taught me that there are several major problems with such a "top-down" approach to Knowledge Management.

It takes a *lot* of time and effort to articulate one's knowledge in a form that can be understood by others. Since most staff aren't compensated or evaluated for that effort, it always tends to fall by the wayside. There are also risks to sharing your ideas openly, from the fear of being criticized or misinterpreted to the possibility that by documenting what you know you'll easily be replaced.

Seeing the top-down approach to KM fail countless times has led me to conclude that a "bottom-up" approach is needed for modern organizations. It can't be about "extracting" knowledge from your people, as if it was a natural resource that could be stockpiled in a warehouse.

Knowledge Management has to be centered on the needs of the individual, designed primarily to enhance their *personal* productivity and effectiveness so they are empowered to do the very best work they are capable of.

Here are my top four recommendations for how to do that using PARA within teams:

1. Get clear on your organization's flavor of PARA

2. Train people in how to use PARA

3. Keep only shared projects on shared platforms

4. Encourage a culture of writing

RECOMMENDATION #1:
Get clear on your organization's flavor of PARA

My first recommendation is to define what PARA looks like for your organization specifically.

Even if you decide to follow my advice to the letter, there is always a "flavor" of PARA that makes sense for your culture.

I suggest creating a "PARA Playbook" for your team that includes decisions such as:

- What is our definition of a "project," "area of responsibility," "resource," and "archive"?
- What needs to happen when we kick off a new project for it to be considered "active"?
- What needs to happen when a project gets completed, put on hold, or canceled (to be considered "inactive")?
- What are the officially supported platforms on which PARA will be used?
- What are the rules, guidelines, and norms that govern how people will use PARA?

- Who will be the "PARA Champion" who oversees its implementation and makes sure the guidelines are being followed?

RECOMMENDATION #2:
Train people in how to use PARA

I suggest you view the implementation of PARA as primarily a *training* challenge, not a technical one.

The biggest pitfall I see managers fall into is the idea that they can "install" PARA without having to teach anyone anything. Nothing could be further from the truth. I promise you: you *will* need to teach your people not only how PARA works, but how it works *for your team*.

I suggest using the PARA Playbook (created per my previous recommendation) to make presentations, run demonstrations, and host workshops to make sure everyone is on board.

Even with such a dead simple method as this one, you will be surprised how many existing habits and mindsets most people have to unlearn in their relationship with information, such as the idea that there is a "right way" to organize; the belief that there is only one place a given piece of information belongs; and the assumption that formal order and precise structure are always better.

Don't skimp on the need to train your colleagues in the shared conventions and policies that will determine how knowledge is created and shared between them.

RECOMMENDATION #3:
Keep only shared projects on shared platforms

As you begin creating a shared PARA across your team or company, look out for a common mistake: moving every single digital asset into a single shared PARA system all at once.

The thinking goes: If this content is so valuable, then shouldn't everyone have access to it?

The answer is no—you absolutely do not want everyone to have access to everything all the time. To understand why, you have to understand that it takes a tremendous amount of cognitive effort to effectively communicate a piece of knowledge.

I once had some personal notes on a book I read about modern project management techniques. They were free-form and messy, since I was the only person who needed to understand them. I wanted to share those insights with my team, but quickly realized that I couldn't simply email them my informal notes. In order for that content to be understandable and relevant, I would need to add *a lot* more context and structure to them: defining key terms, adding headings and sections, including a table of contents, providing more background context, and carefully explaining my thinking.

These kinds of tasks aren't free—they are *cognitively expensive*. They demand a lot of time and effort, which is time and effort not spent moving your top priorities forward. There is always a trade-off.

For that reason, I recommend advising your team to keep all their *personal* notes, files, and documents in their *personal* PARA system by default. Only when a project, area, or resource becomes *collaborative*, with multiple people involved, should it be moved to the shared folders in a company-wide PARA system.

This will ensure that everyone has access only to the information they need to do their jobs, and no more.

● ● ●	**Forte Labs Shared Drive**
▶ 1	Forte Labs Projects
▶ 2	Forte Labs Areas
▶ 3	Forte Labs Resources
▶ 4	Forte Labs Archives

RECOMMENDATION #4:
Encourage a culture of writing

One thing you'll quickly discover is that Knowledge Management is essentially a form of communication.

As I wrote in *Building a Second Brain,* a document, note, or other digital item is a message being sent through time to a future recipient. Like any message, the *quality* of that communication determines whether it is likely to be received and understood on the other end.

A high-quality piece of communication meets the following criteria:

- Is it interesting and attention-grabbing? (Does it make people *want* to read it?)
- Is it precise and clear? (Can people easily understand what it's trying to say?)
- Is it empathetic? (Is it written to be understood from the reader's point of view?)
- Does it help people solve a problem? (Is it clearly useful and effective?)
- Does it inspire people to take action? (Does it make it easy for others to apply it?)

These questions highlight that effective Knowledge Management boils down to how well people express themselves in writing. To put it simply: the only way to share knowledge effectively is to create a culture of writing within your team.

How do you do that? Here are five ideas that I've seen work well:

- **Set an example:** Senior leadership and managers can set an example by regularly sharing their most important ideas and decisions in writing

- **Offer incentives:** Staff at all levels can be rewarded and praised when they take the time to express their thinking in writing
- **Provide feedback:** Direct reports can be offered private feedback on their writing drafts before sharing them more widely
- **Set aside time for reading:** Meetings can begin with "reading time" to emphasize that the context for discussions is best absorbed in written form
- **Standardize:** Adopt a standard term for an internal piece of writing (such as a memo, proposal, one-pager, or article) and create a standard template (such as a Google Doc or Notion page) for doing so

The more encouragement and incentives you offer, the likelier your colleagues are to sit down and compose their ideas in written form. And that habit will lead to higher-quality thinking, better decisions and discussions, and ultimately to more effective Knowledge Management.

3

DEEP DIVES

11

Creating a Project List

I f you were to hire me as your productivity coach, we'd spend
our first few sessions formulating your Project List. That list is
the lynchpin of your productive life, and we can't do much else
without it.

Let me save you that expense by walking you through it now.[13]

Your Project List is a list of the outcomes you are currently
committed to achieving, all in one place. It is an inventory of

---

all the things you're trying to produce, create, accomplish, or resolve.

It's like a to-do list, but on a bigger scale and longer time horizon so you can tell where you're headed. It's like a list of goals, but more practical and rooted in the here and now.

Formulating your Project List is an incredibly useful exercise in its own right, as well as the cornerstone of PARA. Most people find that following the steps below takes five to ten minutes and produces a list of around ten to twenty projects. This is why we want to use a software program to keep track of them—not our brains!

How to Create a Project List:

STEP 1
List all of your current projects

STEP 2
Add a goal for each project

STEP 3
Add deadlines or timeframes

STEP 4
Prioritize your list

STEP 5
Reevaluate your project list

STEP #1:
List Your Current Projects

Set a timer for five minutes (which is enough for a "first pass")
and write down anything that comes to mind when you read the
following questions, whether they are work-related or personal:

- What's currently worrying you?
- What problem is taking more mental bandwidth than
  it deserves?
- What needs to happen that you're not making consistent
  progress on?
- What actions are you already taking that are part of a bigger project you've not yet identified?
- What would you like to learn, develop, build, express, pursue, start, explore, or play with?
- Which skills would you like to learn and which hobbies
  would you like to start?
- What kind of project could advance your career or make
  your life more fun or interesting?

Add a Goal for Each Project

Remember that a project is any endeavor that has:

1. A goal

2. A deadline (or other timeframe)

Take a minute and add a goal for each project on your list in parentheses. For example:

- **Project:** Visit the doctor about back pain (**Goal:** Back pain is resolved and I can sleep through the night without discomfort)

- **Project:** Plan off-site agenda for staff retreat (**Goal:** Team is clear about what needs to be accomplished and next steps are assigned)

- **Project:** Develop sales campaign with Linda (**Goal:** Sales campaign is approved by exec team and budget is allocated)

Add Deadlines or Timeframes

Next, go through the list one more time and add completion dates. Don't get hung up on whether this is a strict "deadline" or simply the date by which you prefer to have it done.

You can add dates to each item on your list by adding "by . . ." at the end. For example:

- Project: Visit the doctor about back pain **by Friday, Feb. 24** (Goal: Back pain is resolved and I can sleep through the night without discomfort)
- Project: Plan off-site agenda for staff retreat **by end of Q3** (Goal: Team is clear about what needs to be accomplished and next steps are assigned)
- Project: Develop sales campaign with Linda **by next executive meeting** (Goal: Sales campaign is approved by exec team and budget is allocated)

Prioritize Your List

You aren't very likely to make progress on every single project on your list in a given week, or even most of them. The key here is to prioritize *only for the upcoming week.*

For just next week, which projects should be taking up most of your mental bandwidth? Put those at the top. Which ones should be taking up little or none of your bandwidth next week? Put those at the bottom.

Your only goal in a given week is to make progress on a handful of projects near the top of that list.

STEP #5:
Reevaluate Your Project List

Now that you have a full inventory of everything you're committed to this week, you have the chance to ask some difficult but incredibly illuminating questions of yourself:

- Which goals or priorities you say are important to you don't have any projects associated with them? (These are called "dreams," since they aren't likely to happen in the near term.)

- Which projects you're spending a lot of time on don't have any goals associated with them? (These are called "hobbies," because without a goal in mind, they are likely "just for fun.")

- Which projects can you cancel, postpone, reduce in scope, delegate, outsource, or clarify?

There's absolutely nothing wrong with dreams and hobbies, by the way. They are just as important and necessary parts of our lives, but don't confuse them with your projects and areas.

All we're doing is aligning where your time and energy are going with what is truly important to you. In the bustle of daily life it's too easy to let them drift out of alignment. Before we know it, we're neglecting everything we claim matters most to us, while pouring our precious time into things we know aren't important at all.

The five steps I've just taken you through can become part of a "weekly review." You can walk through them once a week, or anytime you feel overwhelmed or stretched too thin, and I guarantee you'll emerge in minutes with a newfound sense of clarity and purpose.

Saying Yes and No with Integrity

Creating an accurate Project List gives you the confidence to say yes *or* no to new commitments. Once you know how much capacity you actually have, the decision of what to fill it with can be intentional and strategic, instead of reactive.

Often, my coaching clients' takeaway from performing this exercise is that they are trying to do too much. Seeing the range of their existing commitments all in one place, they realize that they don't need another productivity app or technique—they need to say no to things that don't matter.

When you take the steps needed to clarify what you're most committed to, you can start to make calm, considered decisions about what stays and what needs to go.

And every time you say no to something that is less important, all the time and energy that it was taking up gets freed up for the things that are more important.

12

The Three Core Habits of Organization

H ere's a hard truth: you will most likely forget everything you've read in this book very soon.

This is the whole reason we save things in the first place, isn't it? We know our memories are weak, so we outsource remembering to technology as insurance against that fact.

Instead of pretending like you will remember everything I've written here, let's just assume that within a few hours or days of reading this book, it will become nothing more than a faint memory.

The only thing that will remain is the habits you adopt or change as a result of the advice I've given you.

After seeing how many people implement PARA for themselves, I've identified the three habits that encapsulate everything in this book. Each one is based on a timeless principle that will remain relevant even as the underlying technology changes. Together, they will ensure that you not only *get* organized but *stay* organized far into the future.

THE THREE HABITS:

1

Organize according to outcomes

2

Organize just in time

3

Keep things informal

HABIT #1:
Organize According to Outcomes

One of the biggest pitfalls in organizing is to treat it as an end in itself.

There's something so satisfying about neatly arranging your workspace or designing beautiful notes that look like they belong on Instagram.

There's nothing wrong with those things if you enjoy them, but I don't think that's why you picked up this book. I'm willing to bet there's something you're committed to achieving—a result or outcome that would be meaningful for you.

This is exactly what PARA is designed for:

- Every decision is made through the lens of "What will help me move this forward?"

- All the up-front work of meticulous tagging and labeling and titling is eliminated.

- There's no maintenance required, except getting your projects done.

- The most actionable category of "Projects" is closely guarded against distractions from other kinds of information that seem interesting but aren't useful.

Each of these guardrails is designed to help you eliminate everything that doesn't advance the goal you're striving toward.

Whether you are trying to reach the finish line of a challenging project or striving to elevate your standards in an area of life, always begin with the end in mind and work backward to decide *only* which information you'll need to get there, and push everything else aside.

HABIT #2:
Organize Just in Time

My organizing philosophy is to organize as little as possible, as late as possible, and only as much as absolutely needed.

This may be a strange thing to say in a book about organizing, but organizing by itself doesn't add value. It has no inherent worth unless it puts you in a state of mind for taking effective action.

This is why PARA is a minimalistic approach—it opts for little "nudges" to move items from one place to another as your needs change. It is a "bottom-up" method, responding to changes in your life organically.

Instead of spending a lot of effort organizing your digital information "just in case" you need it someday, wait until your needs become crystal clear and then organize your notes and files "just in time" for the project you're working on *right now*. This is how you avoid doing a lot of up-front work of questionable value, saving your energy for the moment when you know exactly what you're trying to accomplish.

HABIT #3:
Keep Things Informal

PARA requires precision in only one place: the definition of projects. Everything else is not only allowed to remain somewhat messy; that's how it should be. Highly precise systems require a lot of effort to maintain, which means most aspects of your digital world should remain loose and informal by default.

This rule recognizes that imposing order on information doesn't always make it more valuable. You heard that right: sometimes organizing information too much makes it *less* valuable. The greatest breakthroughs often come from unexpected connections between ideas, and if your system is too rigidly formal, you'll prevent such connections from ever forming. Allowing some messiness and randomness into the system creates opportunities for very different ideas to be connected and intermixed.

This is why I don't agree with a lot of the recommendations made by organizing gurus. For example, I don't recommend:

- Creating an internal structure inside folders
- Using a standardized template for the contents of notes or documents
- Creating a hierarchy of subfolders within subfolders many levels deep
- Using databases or other formal methods for organizing personal information

I've tried all these practices in the past, but always found that they took up valuable time that was much better suited to engaging with the ideas themselves. Resist the urge to create overly complex mechanisms where simple, straightforward ones will suffice. Your future self will thank you for saving them all the time-consuming effort such mechanisms always require.

Protecting Your Ideas until They Have Time to Bloom

When a new idea is first forming, it is highly vulnerable. Like an infant, it has a lot of potential but needs to be protected from all kinds of risks and threats—the threat of self-doubt, the risk of being criticized by others, and your own fear that it isn't good enough. The idea can't survive on its own yet, but that doesn't mean it's a bad idea. It just needs time and space to develop to its ultimate potential, just like us humans.

Each habit I've recommended above helps create an environment where such new ideas can emerge. Organizing ideas according to outcomes ensures you're actively testing them in the real world. Organizing just in time preserves your time and energy so you can pursue unexpected opportunities. And keeping things informal by default allows novel connections and patterns to form.

Think of the folders of PARA as a series of protected spaces for fledgling ideas to play in before they grow up.

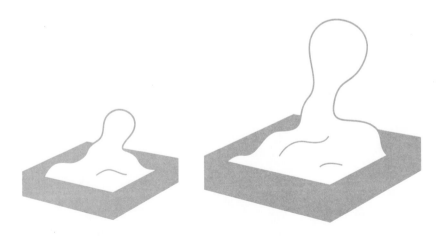

The "walls" of each folder contain a messy sandbox where loosely related ideas can mix together and play. Eventually, they will grow up and become strong enough to venture out into the world on their own.

13

Using PARA to Enhance Focus, Creativity, and Perspective

P ARA can be used to cultivate three of the most desirable states of mind for knowledge workers: focus, creativity, and a sense of perspective.

Let me walk you through each one.

How to Use PARA to Enhance Focus

The very essence of focus is to "do one thing at a time." This principle seems so simple in theory, but in practice it's not so easy.

I've noticed that often people try to focus in the very same environment where new information arrives.

They use their email inbox as a to-do list, then wonder why they're constantly distracted by one incoming message after another. Or they use their web browser to multitask, then can't figure out why at the end of the day they're left with dozens of unread browser tabs.

In order to focus, we need to step away from the incessant notifications of the Internet and withdraw to a private, secluded place.

If you happen to have access to a log cabin hidden deep in the woods, then I'm envious of you. For the rest of us, that private place can be simply a different software program than the one we use to interface with the outside world.

When I need to focus, I turn off the Wi-Fi. I know I can't remain dedicated to one task with an ocean of information beckoning to me from just the other side of a browser window. Each time I sit down to work, I choose a task from my to-do list, turn on "airplane mode" on all my devices, and don't go back online until it's finished.

You might have heard this advice before, but it's almost impossible to follow until you have a trusted, comprehensive system for managing digital information. If everything is stuck in the cloud, you'll never be able to pull away from the siren song of the web and actually get things done.

Use PARA as your secluded log cabin in the woods—a place where you can shut out the world and tinker with your own ideas, theories, and creations before venturing back out to share them with the world.

How to Use PARA to Cultivate Creativity

You've probably heard many times how important creativity is to modern career success.

Collecting information is easy, and we've seen that filing it away isn't that hard either. But if you stop there, all this effort amounts to hoarding. Value doesn't come from the inputs; it comes from your outputs, bearing your signature and style.

A lot of what I write about in *Building a Second Brain* builds on PARA with a holistic system for creativity in the digital age.

But for the purposes of this book, PARA is about creating an environment in which creativity can emerge. Creativity is often mysterious, but one thing I know for sure:

When you have
a collection of
interesting ideas,
thoughtfully
curated, all related
to a single project or
goal and collected
in one central place,
magical things
begin to happen.

Any other creative tool or technique you might want to try will work far better when you have this "starting batch" of material to work with.

To take advantage of this fact, I recommend choosing what to save in your PARA system based on what *resonates* with you. What moves you? What makes the hair stand up on your arm, gives you goose bumps, makes your heart beat faster, or fills you with a sense of wonder? That is the stuff creativity is made of, and therefore worth saving.

How to Use PARA to Give You a Sense of Perspective

It's helpful to think of each main category of PARA as a "horizon."

Your projects exist on a short-term horizon that will play out in the coming hours or days. Your areas of responsibility and resources play out on a medium-term horizon over weeks and months. Your archives are more likely to be useful on a long-term horizon of months or years.

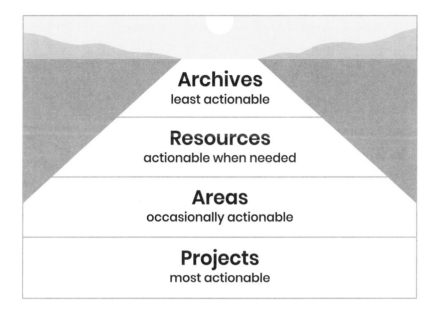

Why is it useful to segment your information based on different timescales? Because each timescale requires a very different mindset and way of thinking.

Day to day, in the trenches of getting things done, you want to focus only on your active projects. Projects include actions that need to be taken and information that needs to be reviewed in the next few hours or days. At this timescale, things are changing fast, so you should keep that information close at hand and at the center of your attention.

These are the kinds of questions that are relevant on this short-term horizon:

- Which projects are most active right now?
- Which tasks are most time-sensitive?
- What are the next steps you need to take to move them forward?
- What information do you need access to in order to do so?

Areas and resources become relevant on a longer time horizon, stretching from weeks to months. You may not need to refer to them much during the workweek, when you're just fighting fires. But occasionally, such as during a weekly review, it's wise to elevate your perspective and think about the long term. This is when the content you've collected in your areas of responsibility and resources becomes valuable.

At these times of deeper reflection, ask yourself these questions:

- What is the standard (of quality or performance) I'm committed to in each of my areas of responsibility?

- Am I currently meeting that standard?
- If not, are there any new projects, habits, routines, or other practices I can start, stop, or change?
- Are there any resources that would enable me to do so?

When evaluating your resources, ask yourself questions like:

- Are there any new interests or passions I'd like to pursue more seriously?
- Are there any curiosities or questions I'd like to start exploring?
- Are there any hobbies or pursuits I've allowed to stagnate that I'd like to reboot?

By separating out the information in your life according to *when it will be needed*, PARA gives you a sense of perspective appropriate to whichever time horizon is calling for your attention. It allows you to work simultaneously across different timescales to bring into existence the future you're trying to create.

14

When in Doubt, Start Over

'*ve offered a lot of advice and recommendations about how to make PARA work for you, and in this chapter I want to give you one final one:

If you ever get stuck or feel overwhelmed, simply archive everything and start over following the instructions I provided in chapter 3. For example:

- If your **Documents folder becomes a digital dumpster fire,** move everything into an archive with today's date and start fresh.

- If you have **tons of digital notes** piled up in the inbox of your notetaking app, move them to an archive folder with today's date and be done with it.

- If your **cloud storage drive is a hot mess,** move everything to a dated archive and reset for a new week, month, or year.

Yes, you read that right: the act of declaring "digital bankruptcy" is an escape hatch that you can use anytime your digital world starts to become too chaotic and suffocating. I've done it countless times, and every time it fills me with a sense of relief and enthusiasm for what's next.

When it comes to your finances, there are serious consequences to declaring bankruptcy. But not in the digital world. There is no downside to archiving everything because it will all remain available in the future.

Everything Is Optional

In this book I've outlined the exact process I follow to keep my own PARA system running, but I want to emphasize that all the steps I've described are optional. None of them are absolutely essential to get value from organizing your digital world.

Some weeks, I'm too busy to review my inboxes and add titles, so I don't. I know that I can always find what I need using search, which doesn't require any manual effort.

Some weeks I'm too busy to individually move each item from the inbox into the right folders, so I just "select all" and dump them anywhere. Again, search is the magic solution to finding things even if they haven't been perfectly classified and labeled.

Finally, there are times when things are so crazy, I don't update my Project List for many weeks at a time. It doesn't matter—I promise there won't be a catastrophe just because there are a few inactive projects lingering on your list.

PARA is highly resilient, and it will preserve everything just as you left it until the day arrives when you have time to reset, whether that's in seven days or seven months. That's the whole point of using a simple system—it easily withstands the passage of time until you're ready to return to it.

Letting Go of Our Attachment to Information

Most of us seem to have a sense of duty toward our digital possessions. From a young age, your parents probably taught you to care for your belongings and treat them with respect. It almost feels like a moral obligation to meticulously upkeep our digital environment the same way we tidy our physical surroundings.

But this attitude makes no sense in the digital world. Trying to preserve every last bit of data is like a hoarder trying to keep every old trinket and empty pizza box in their home. Most of this content appeared without our consent, and therefore we can archive it away without a sense of attachment.

I know archiving everything and starting over can be a scary step. You might have spent years thinking about how you wanted to organize all these files, and now I'm telling you to dump them all into the Archive? Yes, that's exactly what I'm telling you to do.

Remember: you aren't losing anything. If you really need something from the past, you are always free to dive into your Archives and resurrect it. I'm guessing, however, that you'll do so far less than you expect, if ever.

The truth is, search technology is getting better every year, and the most likely way you'll access your files in the future is through increasingly advanced search algorithms. Artificial intelligence is also on the way, which means that in the future you'll probably just ask an AI to search through all your old information and find what you need. That's why any time you spend meticulously organizing your stuff is likely to be wasted.

This is your chance to draw a line in the sand and leave your old relationship with information behind.

It is an opportunity
to assert your digital
independence from
the clutter and mess
keeping you stuck
in the past.

I'm inviting you to embrace a new identity—to become the kind of person who refuses to get bogged down in trivial details and instead embraces what's new and alive in your life right now.

Will you accept my invitation?

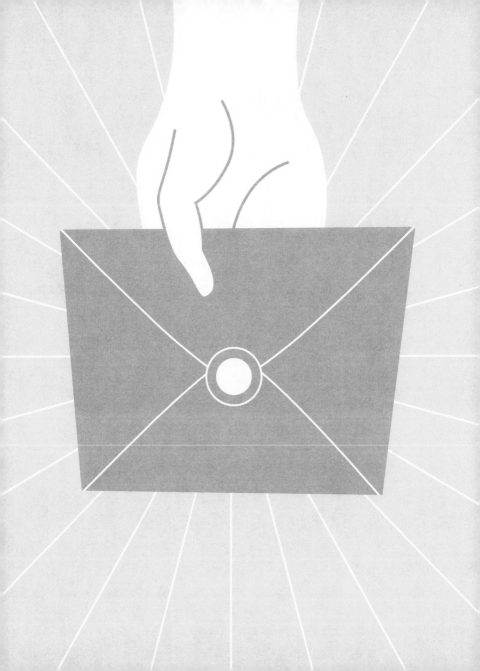

15

Organizing as Personal Growth

Often in my work with coaching clients, I hear some version of this story hidden in their words: "I'm just not organized."

Strangely enough, it tends to be the most competent, productive, and accomplished people who say this. If they weren't driven to achieve more in their lives, then "not being organized" wouldn't be a problem!

We seem to have this subconscious belief that "If I could just get organized, I could achieve anything." Yet when I inquire further, no one seems to have any idea what it really means to "get organized." It is a mirage, always teasing us from a distance, but even when we move toward it, it remains as distant as ever.

I have a definition of "getting organized" that I want to share with you. But first let's talk about what it's not.

Getting organized is not about aesthetics, or the way things look. Don't be lured into believing that a workspace full of squared edges, clean lines, and minimalistic whitespace will somehow magically grant you clarity or peace of mind.

Getting organized is not about control. Don't fall into the trap of trying to rigidly control your digital environment as an excuse to avoid facing the inherent uncertainty of life.

Getting organized, in my opinion, is about acquiring power.

"Power" is a dirty word for many people. We're not supposed to *want* power. That's a shameful desire best left to corrupt politicians and greedy capitalists, right?

Wrong.

Everything you want depends on how much power you have. All the goals you have for your career and your family, all the change you want to cause in your field or your community, all the relationships you want to form or improve, all the things you want to experience and possess.

It all depends on your ability to draw power from every source available to you and direct it toward the outcomes you want.

Power comes from the strength of your intellect. This is why I advise you to consume ideas from the world's best thinkers and save the best ones you encounter in a centralized place that you can access anytime.

Power comes from the force of your emotions. By surrounding yourself with information that provokes a feeling of fascination, you'll begin to harness the incredible enthusiasm for learning and growth you have trapped inside.

Power comes from systems that don't depend on your energy levels, attention span, or self-discipline. That's why PARA asks you to make one decision for each piece of information, and one decision only: When will this be relevant next?

Finally, power comes from alignment.

There is a common temptation to set up PARA to resemble the life you *wish you had*, instead of the life you actually have. Don't create a bunch of aspirational projects and goals that are merely wishful thinking. When you have the courage to tell the truth about what is truly occupying your attention right now, and make PARA reflect that, the power really begins to flow.

You can't change anything until you're completely honest with yourself about what needs changing.

The Era of the Wisdom Worker

For decades, we've called ourselves "knowledge workers" based on the fact that knowledge was our main asset.

More than sixty years after that term was coined, the era of the knowledge worker is finally coming to a close. Knowledge has been commoditized and made universally accessible, first through search engines and now through increasingly advanced artificial intelligence. Which means there is no advantage to knowing any particular piece of knowledge anymore.

We are now entering the era of the Wisdom Worker.

What matters now is the ability to elevate your perspective above the fray of the day-to-day noise, remain in a place of calm perspective, and from that place to orchestrate the people, systems, tools, and flows of information surging around you.

We encounter reality as a chaotic stream of information flowing around and through us at all times. It doesn't arrive in preformed units, neatly labeled as "projects" or "areas." You are the one who reaches out and carves out chunks of information to make your own. You have the choice to grasp only the pieces that move you and make you feel alive.

Often as people begin working with PARA they realize that they already have more than enough knowledge to pursue the goal they've been dreaming of.

When you see all
the valuable raw
material you've
already collected,
whether from your
own experience or
the experiences of
others, all in one
place, you can't help
but conclude that

you're ready.

What is that dream for you? What have you been telling yourself you'll be ready for in a month, or a year, or three years, or five years that, if you're really honest with yourself, you are ready for today?

The promise of PARA is that it makes "getting organized" a straightforward affair to get over with as quickly as possible. It is a way to step out from behind your computer screen and out into the world where all the possibilities reside. It is a way to tap into the sources of power available all around you so you can fulfill the purpose you were put on this planet for.